LET'S EXPLORE THE STATES

Gulf States

Alabama
Louisiana
Mississippi

John Ziff

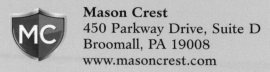

Mason Crest
450 Parkway Drive, Suite D
Broomall, PA 19008
www.masoncrest.com

©2016 by Mason Crest, an imprint of National Highlights, Inc.

Printed and bound in the United States of America.

CPSIA Compliance Information: Batch #LES2015.
For further information, contact Mason Crest at 1-866-MCP-Book.

First printing
1 3 5 7 9 8 6 4 2

Library of Congress Cataloging-in-Publication Data

Ziff, John.
  Gulf states : Alabama, Louisiana, Mississippi / John Ziff.
    pages cm. — (Let's explore the states)
  Includes bibliographical references and index.
  ISBN 978-1-4222-3324-5 (hc)
  ISBN 978-1-4222-8609-8 (ebook)
  1. Gulf States—Juvenile literature. 2. Alabama—Juvenile literature.
  3. Louisiana—Juvenile literature. 4. Mississippi—Juvenile literature. I. Title.
  F296.Z54 2015
  976—dc23

                              2014050183

Let's Explore the States series ISBN: 978-1-4222-3319-1

Publisher's Note: Websites listed in this book were active at the time of publication. The publisher is not responsible for websites that have changed their address or discontinued operation since the date of publication. The publisher reviews and updates the websites each time the book is reprinted.

About the Author: John Ziff is an editor and writer. He lives near Philadelphia.

Picture Credits: Library of Congress: 15, 16, 17, 19 (top right), 20 (top), 32, 35, 36 (bottom), 39 (left), 51, 52, 55, 58 (top and center); National Park Service: 34; used under license from Shutterstock, Inc.: 1, 3, 6, 9, 10, 11 (top), 12, 18, 24, 26, 29 (top left and right, bottom left), 30, 36 (top), 37, 39 (right), 40, 42 (left), 43, 44, 46, 53, 57 (top), 59, 60; 360b/Shutterstock: 20 (bottom); Action Sports Photography/Shutterstock: 22; Allen Berezovsky/Shutterstock: 58 (bottom); S. Bukley / Shutterstock.com: 42 (right, top and center); Featureflash/Shutterstock: 42 (right, bottom); Anton Foltin/Shutterstock: 49 (bottom left); Steven Frame/Shutterstock: 19 (bottom right); Zack Frank/Shutterstock: 50; Karen Foley Photography / Shutterstock.com: 33; Rob Hainer / Shutterstock.com: 19 (bottom left), 21, 49 (top right), 57 (bottom); Danny E. Hooks/Shutterstock: 23 (bottom); Matthew Jacques/Shutterstock: 38; Wayne James/Shutterstock: 11 (bottom); Ed Metz/Shutterstock: 49 (bottom right); John Panella/Shutterstock: 61; Catalin Petolea/Shutterstock: 49 (top left); Jason Patrick Ross/Shutterstock: 23 (top); Spirit of America/Shutterstock: 56; Katherine Welles/Shutterstock: 48; Gary Yim/Shutterstock: 29 (bottom, right); U.S. Navy photo courtesy Austal USA: 19 (top left).

Table of Contents

KEY ICONS TO LOOK FOR:

Words to Understand: These words with their easy-to-understand definitions will increase the reader's understanding of the text, while building vocabulary skills.

Sidebars: This boxed material within the main text allows readers to build knowledge, gain insights, explore possibilities, and broaden their perspectives by weaving together additional information to provide realistic and holistic perspectives.

Research Projects: Readers are pointed toward areas of further inquiry connected to each chapter. Suggestions are provided for projects that encourage deeper research and analysis.

Text-Dependent Questions: These questions send the reader back to the text for more careful attention to the evidence presented there.

Series Glossary of Key Terms: This back-of-the book glossary contains terminology used throughout this series. Words found here increase the reader's ability to read and comprehend higher-level books and articles in this field.

LET'S EXPLORE THE STATES

Atlantic: North Carolina, Virginia, West Virginia
Central Mississippi River Basin: Arkansas, Iowa, Missouri
East South-Central States: Kentucky, Tennessee
Eastern Great Lakes: Indiana, Michigan, Ohio
Gulf States: Alabama, Louisiana, Mississippi
Lower Atlantic: Florida, Georgia, South Carolina
Lower Plains: Kansas, Nebraska
Mid-Atlantic: Delaware, District of Columbia, Maryland
Non-Continental: Alaska, Hawaii
Northern New England: Maine, New Hampshire, Vermont
Northeast: New Jersey, New York, Pennsylvania
Northwest: Idaho, Oregon, Washington
Rocky Mountain: Colorado, Utah, Wyoming
Southern New England: Connecticut, Massachusetts, Rhode Island
Southwest: New Mexico, Oklahoma, Texas
U.S. Territories and Possessions
Upper Plains: Montana, North Dakota, South Dakota
West: Arizona, California, Nevada
Western Great Lakes: Illinois, Minnesota, Wisconsin

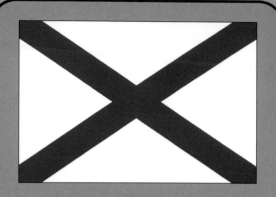

Alabama at a Glance

Area: 52,420 sq mi (135,767 sq km).[1]
   30th largest state
   Land: 50,645 sq mi (131,170 sq km)
   Water: 1,775 sq mi (4,597 sq km)
Highest elevation: Cheaha
   Mountain, 2,407 feet (734 m)
Lowest elevation: Gulf of Mexico,
   sea level

Statehood: December 14, 1819
   (22nd state)
Capital: Montgomery

Population: 4,849,377
   (23rd largest state)[2]

State nickname: the Heart of Dixie
State bird: yellowhammer (northern
   flicker)
State flower: camellia

[1] U.S. Census Bureau
[2] U.S. Census Bureau, 2014 estimate

Alabama

The term *Dixie* refers to the South—and specifically to the states that broke away from the Union and sparked the Civil War in 1861. Alabama is often called "the Heart of Dixie." It lay at the geographic center of the Confederate States of America. That was the new nation formed by the 11 breakaway states. Alabama was where the Confederate constitution was adopted. Montgomery, Alabama, served as the first Confederate capital. Yet Alabama isn't defined only by its role in the Civil War. The "Heart of Dixie" was also a key battleground in the struggle for civil rights.

Geography

Alabama has borders with four other states. Mississippi lies to the west. Tennessee forms Alabama's northern border. Georgia is to the east, and Florida to the south. Alabama also has a 53-mile coastline along the Gulf of Mexico. This is in the southwestern part of the state. Three islands in the Gulf belong to Alabama.

Alabama is the nation's 30th largest state by total area. It covers more than 52,400 square miles (135,000 square kilometers).

More than half of Alabama is made up of *coastal plain*. This low, flat or gently rolling land begins in the southernmost part of the state. It extends to the middle of Alabama in the east. In the west, the coastal plain stretches farther north. It nearly reaches the border with Tennessee in the far western part of Alabama.

Cutting across Alabama's coastal plain and into Mississippi is a region known as the ***Black Belt***. Its rich, dark soil is excellent for farming.

North of the coastal plain, in the eastern part of the state, is a wedge-shaped area of uplands occupying less than 10 percent of Alabama. It's the southernmost part of the Piedmont, a ***plateau*** region to the east of the Appalachian Mountains. The Piedmont

Words to Understand in This Chapter

annex—to take possession of territory and incorporate it into an existing country or state.

Black Belt—a region of central Alabama and Mississippi that has dark, fertile soil and that was previously home to many large cotton plantations.

boycott—a mass refusal to buy a product, use a service, or have other dealings with an organization, with the goal of pressuring the organization to change its practices.

civil rights movement—an extended effort, conducted largely during the 1950s and 1960s, to secure for African Americans the rights of personal liberty guaranteed to all citizens.

coastal plain—an area of flat, mostly low-lying land that extends inland from a seacoast.

plateau—an area of relatively flat land that is raised sharply above adjacent land on at least one side.

poll tax—a sum of money that must be paid in order to be eligible to vote.

secede—to withdraw from a political union.

segregation—the practice of keeping white and black people apart in public.

tableland—a plateau.

Although the crop no longer dominates its economy, Alabama consistently ranks among the top 10 U.S. states in annual cotton production.

cuts through eight states in all. Alabama's Piedmont section is flat in the south. But in the north, it's fairly rugged. Cheaha Mountain, Alabama's highest point, is located in this area. It rises more than 2,400 feet (734 m) above sea level in Cleburne County.

To the northwest of Alabama's Piedmont lies a region of sharp ridges and narrow valleys making up about 9 percent of the state. The ridges and valleys generally run in a northeast-to-southwest direction, but some are quite irregular.

The Cumberland Plateau covers all of northeastern Alabama and extends

Noccalula Falls in Gadsden is part of the northeastern Appalachian Ridge and Valley region. This area is rich in mineral resources and provides Alabama with much of the raw material needed for manufacturing iron and steel.

southwest toward the central part of the state. In all, it accounts for about 15 percent of Alabama's total area. The Cumberland Plateau isn't unbroken **tableland**. Rather, it's a series of plateau areas interrupted by steep valleys. The highest elevations—up to 1,800 feet (549 m)—occur in the northeast. From there the land gradually gets lower as it stretches toward the coastal plain.

A small region in north and northwest Alabama consists of low mountains and valleys. Elevations range from about 400 feet (122 m) to about 900 feet (274 m). Much of this region falls within the Tennessee Valley. It contains excellent farmland.

Alabama has abundant freshwater resources, including 17 major river systems. Among the biggest are the Alabama, Chattahoochee, Tennessee, and Tombigbee. Alabama has no natural lakes. But dams have created many manmade ones. Covering more than 100 square miles (259 sq km), Guntersville Lake is the largest.

Alabama has a warm and humid climate. Winters are mild. On a typical January day in Mobile, in the southern

A covered bridge at Green Mountain Nature Trail, a popular park in Madison County.

Wilson Dam, shown here with its floodgates open, is located on the Tennessee River near Florence. At 137 feet (42 m) high and 4,541 feet (1,384 m) long, it's the largest conventional hydroelectric facility in the Tennessee Valley Authority (TVA) system.

part of the state, the low temperature is about 40° Fahrenheit (4° Celsius) and the high temperature reaches around 60°F (16°C). Average January temperatures in Huntsville, in northern Alabama, are about 10°F cooler. In the summer, both cities experience average high temperatures of 85°F (29°C) or higher. Rainfall is abundant year round. Statewide, annual precipitation averages about 58 inches (147 cm), making Alabama one of the wettest states.

History

Before the arrival of white settlers, various Indian groups occupied what is today Alabama. The Creek (or Muskogee) Confederacy was an alliance of town-dwelling peoples from various tribes. Other important tribes were the Choctaw, Chickasaw, and Cherokee.

The first Europeans to explore what is today Alabama were Spanish. Hernando de Soto's 600-man force trekked through the area in 1539–1540. They wreaked considerable havoc among the Indian population.

More than 150 years would pass before a permanent European settlement had been established in present-day Alabama. In 1702, the French built a fort along the Mobile River, 27

The French built Fort Conde at Mobile in 1717. It helped to maintain French rule in the South and served as a military headquarters until 1763. Parts of the fort were rebuilt in 1976 as part of the national bicentennial celebration. Today, the restored fort functions as a museum.

miles (43 km) north of Mobile Bay. Nine years later, the settlement was moved south, to the site of present-day Mobile. It served as the capital of French Louisiana—a huge territory in the middle of North America claimed by France—until 1720.

The Gulf Coast region between Florida in the east and the Mississippi River in the west changed hands several times during the 1700s. Great Britain claimed possession of the region in 1763. The British had defeated France in the Seven Years' War (known in North America as the French and Indian War). Britain ceded the area to Spain in 1783, after the United States had won independence in the Revolutionary War. The United States gained most of the area through a 1795 treaty with Spain. Spain kept the Mobile District, a small area in present-day southeastern Mississippi and southwestern Alabama.

In 1798, the U.S. Congress organized the Mississippi Territory. It consisted of a slice of present-day Alabama and Mississippi extending

 Did You Know?

On October 18, 1540, Hernando de Soto's Spanish force fought a huge battle with Indian warriors led by a chief named Tuskaloosa. The battle took place somewhere in western or southwestern Alabama, at an Indian town known as Mabila. The Spaniards suffered only about 20 dead while killing thousands of Indians and burning Mabila to the ground. Still, many historians believe de Soto's expedition never fully recovered from the battle. The Spaniards lost a lot of their horses and equipment at Mabila, and many of the men were wounded.

only about a hundred miles (161 km) from south to north. In 1804, however, the Mississippi Territory was expanded to the current northern borders of Alabama and Mississippi. In 1812, the United States *annexed* the Mobile District. That area was added to the Mississippi Territory.

In 1813–1814, the Creek War raged across parts of present-day Alabama, Georgia, and Florida. It began as a sort of civil war within the Creek Confederacy. The conflict widened and grew more brutal after Americans sided with one Creek group against the other, called the Red Sticks. More than 2,000 people had been killed before the Red Sticks were finally defeated at the Battle of Horseshoe Bend. That battle took place in what is today central Alabama on March 27, 1814.

Andrew Jackson had been in command of the American forces at Horseshoe Bend. On August 9, 1814, Jackson compelled the Creeks to sign a harsh treaty. The Treaty of Fort Jackson took about 23 million acres (9 million hectares) of Creek land—including nearly 8 million acres (3 millon ha) from Creeks who'd been allied with the United States. The treaty opened up central Alabama to white settlement.

Years later, Andrew Jackson would be elected president of the United States. During the 1830s, he oversaw the forced removal of the Creek, Cherokee, Chickasaw, Choctaw, and Seminole tribes to land west of the Mississippi River.

In 1817, Mississippi gained statehood, and the Alabama Territory was organized. Two years later, on December 14, 1819, Alabama became the 22nd state.

The 1820 census counted more than 144,000 Alabamians. A third of them were slaves. By 1850, Alabama had more than 340,000 slaves—nearly 45 percent of the state's total population. Alabama was a major cotton-growing state, with plantations concentrated in the Black Belt and Tennessee Valley regions. Slavery made the huge cotton plantations profitable.

Over the course of the 1800s, slavery had become an increasingly explosive issue in the United States. Many in the North were determined to see it ended. Southerners were equally determined to maintain—or even expand—it.

Matters finally came to a head after the 1860 election of Abraham Lincoln as president of the United States. Lincoln was against slavery. But he'd been careful to say he would not try to do away with slavery where it already existed. This wasn't enough for many Southerners. Eleven Southern states *seceded*, or withdrew, from the United States. Seven of them, including Alabama, did so before Lincoln had even taken office. The Civil War resulted.

In February 1861, the Confederate States of America was founded in Montgomery. The city served as the Confederate capital for the next three months.

During the four years of the Civil War, as many as 120,000 Alabamians

The Battle of Mobile Bay in August 1864 was an important Union victory. A U.S. naval fleet commanded by Admiral David G. Farragut sailed through a narrow channel to capture the port, despite the danger of floating mines (called torpedoes at the time) and powerful gunfire from nearby Fort Morgan. Mobile had been the last major seaport open in the Confederacy, and with its capture the Southern cause was doomed.

Alabama's first African-American congressman was Benjamin S. Turner (1825–1894). Born into slavery, Turner was freed during the Civil War. He was elected to the U.S. House of Representatives in 1870, and served a two-year term.

took up arms for the Confederacy. They suffered heavy casualties, including an estimated 25,000 dead. But Alabama was largely spared the devastation that Southern states such as Virginia and Georgia endured. Few battles were fought on Alabama soil.

The Confederates surrendered in 1865. The period that followed is known as Reconstruction. It lasted about a dozen years. During that time, the U.S. Congress tried to reorganize the Southern states and make sure newly freed blacks enjoyed full citizenship rights.

Alabama was readmitted into the Union in 1868, after passing a constitution that allowed black men to vote for the first time in the state's history.

Also for the first time, Alabama established a system of public education. It benefited black children as well as poor white children.

But, in a pattern that was repeated throughout the South, the gains Alabama's blacks had made were soon reversed. African Americans (as well as poor whites) were prevented from voting by the adoption of a **poll tax**. Laws were passed that required blacks and whites to be **segregated**, or kept apart, in public places. "Separate but equal" accommodations were supposed to be made for black and white people. But invariably the facilities provided for African Americans—the schools their children attended, the restaurant areas where they could eat, the restrooms they could use, and much more—were not equal. They were inferior to the facilities whites enjoyed. This system of legal segregation was known as Jim Crow, and it helped ensure that African Americans would be second-class citizens.

Jim Crow existed from the late 1800s to the early 1960s. One of the first major blows to the system was struck in Montgomery, Alabama. On December 1, 1955, an African-American woman named Rosa Parks refused to give up her bus seat to a white passenger and move to the back of the bus, as the law required. She was arrested.

In response, civil rights leaders organized a **boycott** of Montgomery's buses. African Americans refused to ride the buses until the policy of segregated seating was changed. The Montgomery Bus Boycott went on for months. Finally, in December 1956, the U.S. Supreme Court ordered the city—as well as the rest of Alabama—to stop reserving seats for white passengers. The victory inspired supporters of civil rights across the country.

Alabama was the scene of another landmark event in the **civil rights movement**. On March 7, 1965, about 600 demonstrators started out on a planned march from Selma to the state capitol in Montgomery. They wanted to draw attention to Alabama's continuing efforts to prevent African Americans from voting. The marchers had not gone far before state and

On December 1, 1955, Rosa Parks was arrested and charged with disorderly conduct in Montgomery, Alabama, for refusing to give up her bus seat to a white passenger. Her arrest and $14 fine for violating a city ordinance led African-American bus riders and others to boycott the Montgomery city buses. The boycott lasted for one year and brought the civil rights movement worldwide attention.

local police blocked their way and then attacked them savagely. Photographers and television crews recorded the incident, and Americans were repulsed by the police brutality. The incident helped create momentum for the Voting Rights Act, which Congress passed in August 1965.

The Alabama State Capitol in Montgomery was constructed in 1851, although wings were added to the building in subsequent years. In 1861, the building briefly served as the capitol of the Confederate States of America.

Government

Alabama has a bicameral, or two-chamber, legislature. The lower chamber is the 105-seat House of Representatives. Its members are elected to four-year terms. The upper chamber of the Alabama State Legislature is the 35-seat Senate. Senators, too, serve four-year terms. Members of the Alabama Senate and House of Representatives may run for reelection as often as they want.

By contrast, term limits do apply to the Alabama governorship. No one may serve more than two consecutive terms as governor. The length of a term is four years.

In addition to the two U.S. Senate seats allotted to every state, Alabama's congressional delegation includes seven members of the U.S. House of Representatives.

The Economy

Alabama's agricultural economy was once dominated by cotton. While it continues to be an important crop, cotton no longer ranks as the state's most valuable agricultural product. That distinction now belongs to broil-

In recent years, many auto companies have built manufacturing facilities in Alabama, including Honda, Hyundai, and Toyota. Nearly 6,000 people are employed at this Mercedes-Benz plant in Tuscaloosa County.

A U.S. Navy warship, USS Millinocket, awaits delivery at the Austal USA vessel completion yard in Mobile. In recent years Austal, one of the largest shipbuilders on the Gulf Coast, has received multi-billion dollar contracts to build warships for the navy.

The U.S. Space and Rocket Center in Huntsville is a museum dedicated to teaching people about the history of the American space program.

A freighter is loaded at Mobile Harbor, the nation's ninth-largest port. The Alabama State Port Authority reports that approximately 23 million tons of material is shipped through Mobile each year.

er chickens (chickens bred specifically for their meat and harvested at a young age). In 2014, Alabama exported more poultry and poultry products than all but three other states. Alabama also produces cattle and catfish. Peanuts and soybeans are among the leading crops.

Alabama has a significant manufacturing sector. Several foreign auto-

Some Famous Alabamians

Born a slave in Virginia, educator and author Booker T. Washington (1856–1915) would become the leading voice of the African-American community while serving as head of Alabama's Tuskegee Institute.

As a toddler, Helen Keller (1880–1968) was stricken by an illness that left her blind and deaf, but the native of Tuscumbia still became a famous author, lecturer, and political activist.

Oakville-born Jesse Owens (1913–1980) didn't just win four track and field gold medals at the 1936 Berlin Olympics. He discredited the racial theories of Nazi Germany.

In Alabama, the name of Paul "Bear" Bryant (1913–1983) still inspires reverence. The longtime head coach of the Crimson Tide won six national football championships.

Joe Louis

Montgomery resident Rosa Parks (1913–2005) jump-started the civil rights movement in 1955 by refusing to give up her bus seat.

Boxer Joe Louis (1914–1981), who spent his early years in rural Alabama, held the heavyweight title longer than anyone else ever.

Willie Mays (b. 1931) grew up in Westfield, and Hank Aaron (b. 1934) in Mobile. The two are among baseball's greatest players of all time.

Birmingham-born Condoleezza Rice (b. 1954) served as secretary of state under President George W. Bush.

Condoleezza Rice

mobile makers, including Honda, Toyota, and Mercedes-Benz, have assembly plants in the state. These plants, in turn, support numerous auto-parts companies in Alabama.

The aerospace and defense industry—centered primarily in the Huntsville area—is another major employer. Companies located in Alabama also manufacture steel, cast iron, and other metal products.

In spite of its healthy manufacturing base, Alabama is a relatively poor state overall. According to the U.S. Census Bureau, Alabama ranks 44th among all states in income per person.

The People

If you asked a group of Alabamians what they're most passionate about, chances are that at least some of them would say college football. Alabama has no professional sports teams. But it does have a long tradition of great college football teams. The Alabama Crimson Tide claims 15 national football championships. The Auburn Tigers own another two—and in 2014 claimed four other national titles in seasons when there was no undisputed champion. Their triumphs are a source of considerable state pride, though the

The University of Alabama's Crimson Tide football team plays its home games at Bryant-Denny Stadium on the university's campus in Tuscaloosa. The Crimson Tide have won 15 national championships.

The Talladega Superspeedway, used for NASCAR races, is the longest oval track in the country. Each lap is 2.66 miles (4.28 km).

Alabama-Auburn rivalry is intense.

In 2014, the U.S. Census Bureau estimated that there were more than 4.8 million people living in Alabama, making it the 23rd largest state by population. African Americans make up 26.5 percent of Alabama's population. That's more than twice the percentage of blacks in the U.S. population overall. Alabama has a somewhat smaller proportion of whites (70 percent) than the nation as a whole (77.9 percent). It has a far smaller proportion of Latinos (4.1 percent versus 16.9 percent).

Spectacular cave formations at Rickwood Caverns. This state park near Birmingham has more than a mile of underground caverns, where visitors can marvel at 260-million-year-old limestone formations and see blind cave fish swimming in an underground pool.

In the spring of 2010, an oil rig operated by British Petroleum (BP) exploded and sank in the Gulf of Mexico. Over the next three months, more than 210 million gallons of oil spilled into the Gulf, washing onto beaches on the coast of Alabama and other states and causing an environmental catastrophe.

Birmingham, in the foothills of the Appalachian Mountains, is Alabama's largest city and a major industrial center.

Major Cities

With a population of more than 212,000, **Birmingham** is Alabama's largest city. Located in central Alabama's Jefferson County, it was founded in 1871. Birmingham was long a major center of steel production and the South's leading industrial city.

Alabama's capital, **Montgomery**, is situated along the Alabama River in the central part of the state. It has more than 205,000 residents.

About 195,000 people call **Mobile** home. The historic city, located at the northern end of Mobile Bay, is a cultural center. It's also Alabama's only seaport.

Huntsville is nicknamed "the Rocket Capital of the World." That's because the city has played a major role in America's space program. Huntsville is home to NASA's Marshall Space Flight Center. It's located in northern Alabama's Madison County, and is home to more than 180,000 people.

Further Reading

Freedman, Russell. *Freedom Walkers: The Story of the Montgomery Bus Boycott*. New York: Holiday House, 2008.

Philipson, Claire Leila. *Alabama*. Vancouver: Whitecap Books, 2010.

Stallworth, Clarke. *One Day in Alabama: The Civil War Years*. Hoover, AL: Seacoast Publishing, 1997.

Internet Resources

http://www.encyclopediaofalabama.org/face/QuickFacts.jsp

Facts and photos, from the Alabama Humanities Foundation's Encyclopedia of Alabama.

http://www.archives.alabama.gov/

The Web site of Alabama's Department of Archives & History offers a comprehensive timeline, a list of state emblems and symbols, and more.

http://alabama.travel/

Points of interest for visitors to Alabama.

 # Text-Dependent Questions

1. Identify at least two important Indian groups that lived in Alabama.
2. Alabama's oldest city was founded by the French. Can you name the city?

 # Research Project

The city of Enterprise, Alabama, has a monument dedicated to the boll weevil. Find out what the boll weevil is and what role it played in Alabama history. Why would some Alabamians be grateful for the boll weevil?

 Louisiana at a Glance

Area: 52,378 sq mi (135,658 sq km)[1].
  31st largest state
  Land: 43,204 sq mi (111,898 sq km)
  Water: 9,174 sq mi (23,761 sq km)
Highest elevation: Driskill Mountain, 535 feet (163 m)
Lowest elevation: New Orleans, 8 feet (2.4 m) below sea level

Statehood: April 30, 1812 (18th state)
Capital: Baton Rouge

Population: 4,649,676
  (25th largest state)[2]

State nickname: the Pelican State
State bird: eastern brown pelican
State flower: magnolia

[1] U.S. Census Bureau
[2] U.S. Census Bureau, 2014 estimate

Louisiana

Jambalaya is a dish that's very popular in Louisiana. It's made with an array of ingredients. Typically, they include chicken, ham or sausage, shrimp or oysters, celery, peppers, onions, a variety of herbs and spices, hot sauce, rice, and often tomatoes. The ingredients are simmered together. The result is a hearty meal with distinctive flavors.

In some ways, Louisiana is like jambalaya. It's a mixture of many diverse influences—Spanish, French, African, Caribbean, *Cajun*, Native American, British, Irish, and more. Over the course of several centuries, these influences have blended together to create a unique and fascinating culture.

Geography

Louisiana is located on the Gulf Coast, between Mississippi on the east and Texas on the west. Arkansas borders Louisiana to the north.

The 31st largest state by area, Louisiana covers more than 52,000 square miles (135,000 sq km). Of this, more than 9,000 square miles (23,700 sq km) are water. That's about 17.5 percent of Louisiana's total area.

Louisiana's major rivers include the Mississippi, Ouachita, Atchafalaya, Red, and Sabine. Larger lakes include Lake Pontchartrain (which is actually an *estuary* connected to the Gulf of Mexico), Lake Maurepas, Calcasieu Lake, White Lake, and Grand Lake. In addition to its larger bodies of water, Louisiana has numerous streams and creeks, as well as millions of acres of wetlands. The southern part of the state is covered with marshes and *bayous*.

The Mississippi River played a crucial role in shaping Louisiana's land. Over thousands of years, the river deposited silt and nutrients on the surrounding area when it flooded. The *alluvial plain* that resulted has very fertile soil. Before it reaches the Gulf of Mexico, the Mississippi separates into four branches, or passes. This area, the Mississippi River delta, was

Words to Understand in This Chapter

alluvial plain—a lowland area adjacent to a large river upon which sediment is deposited when the river floods.

bayou—a slow-moving creek or a swampy segment of a lake or river.

Cajun—a Louisianan descended from a group of French-speaking people expelled from Acadia (in the present-day Maritime provinces of Canada) during the 18th century.

charter—a grant of rights and privileges from the ruler of a country.

Creole—in Louisiana, a person of mixed French, Spanish, and African heritage; also, a language spoken in Louisiana that combines French and African languages.

estuary—a water passage where the tide meets a river current.

indentured—legally bound or required to work for someone else for a specified period of time.

parish—a unit of local government in Louisiana that is equivalent to a county.

The Louisiana swamp crayfish (or crawfish) is a freshwater crustacean that is eaten or used as fishing bait. Although these creatures are found in running water throughout the United States, Louisiana provides more than 90 percent of all crayfish harvested in the country each year.

Louisiana is known for its cypress swamps and bayous, such as this one at Avery Island.

Aerial view of paddle-wheeled steamboats docked on the Mississippi River at New Orleans.

Celebrating Mardi Gras with a parade in the French Quarter of New Orleans.

Two sailboats silhouetted against the dusky sky as the sun sets over Lake Pontchartrain, an estuary connected to the Gulf of Mexico that covers 630 square miles (1,600 sq km). In the background is the Lake Pontchartrain Causeway, the longest continuous bridge over water in the world.

The brown pelican was designated Louisiana's state bird in 1966.

built up by sediment deposited by the river. The Mississippi River's alluvial plain covers eastern and southeastern Louisiana, about one-quarter of the state in all.

Western Louisiana is made up of coastal plain. Wetlands dominate in the south. Further inland, there are sizable areas of prairie and of pine forests. To the north, the land rises a bit, with some rolling hills. Still, the highest point in the state, Driskill Mountain, is just 535 feet (163 m) above sea level. It's located in Bienville Parish. (A *parish* in Louisiana is like a county in other states.)

Louisiana has a warm, humid climate. Winters are short and mild. Summers are long and hot. A typical January day in New Orleans, which is in the southeastern part of the state, will have a low temperature of about 47°F (8°C) and a high of about 60°F (16°C). In July, the daily low is almost always around 75°F (24°C), and the daily high around 90°F (32°C). In northern Louisiana, temperatures tend to be lower in the winter but a bit higher in the summer.

Louisiana receives abundant precipitation. Rainfall averages more than 60 inches (152 cm) in coastal areas, and about 55 inches (140 cm) in the northern part of the state. It occasionally snows in the north.

Louisiana is subject to frequent severe weather. Florida is the only state that experiences more thunderstorms, and on average Louisiana gets hit by more than 25 tornadoes per year. Tropical storms and hurricanes affecting the state are also common.

History

In 1682, the French explorer René-Robert Cavelier led an expedition down the Mississippi River, from present-day Illinois all the way to the Gulf of Mexico. Cavelier, who is better known by his title Sieur de La Salle, claimed for France the Mississippi River and its entire drainage basin. That massive territory included a million square miles in the center of North America. La Salle dubbed the territory La Louisiane in honor of Louis XIV, king of France.

Of course, the land La Salle

Illustration from a Dutch book, published in 1698, shows the French explorer Robert Cavelier Sieur de La Salle (1643–1687) observing his men unloading supplies during the journey to the Gulf Coast. The explorer claimed an enormous region along the Mississippi River for the French king.

claimed was already occupied by native peoples. But European explorers of the era didn't trouble themselves with such details. At the time, tribes living in what is now the state of Louisiana included the Caddo, Chitimacha, Houma, and Tunica-Biloxi. Other tribes would later move to Louisiana from the east, under pressure from white settlers.

To solidify its claims to the Gulf Coast area, France moved to establish a colony in the region. Its initial settlements came to the east of present-day Louisiana—in the area of Biloxi Bay (present-day Mississippi) and Mobile Bay (Alabama).

Natchitoches, the first French settlement inside present-day Louisiana, was established in 1714. New Orleans was founded four years later. Strategically located on the Mississippi River just south of Lake Pontchartrain, it became the capital of La Louisiane—or French Louisiana—in 1722.

France's colonial enterprise foundered in its early years. More than a decade of direct administration by the French crown proved unsuccessful. A wealthy adviser to Louis XIV, Antoine Crozat, lost a huge sum of money operating French Louisiana under a royal **charter** between 1712 and 1717. The company that succeeded Crozat was bankrupt, and had ruined numerous investors, by 1720. Multiple reorganizations of the company failed to turn the situation around. By 1731, Louisiana had been returned to the crown.

The problems were many. But among the most serious was a shortage of settlers. To boost the population, wealthy Frenchmen received land grants along the Mississippi River above New Orleans. Young women were shipped to Louisiana from French orphanages, convents, and prisons to become settlers' wives. Male convicts were sent to serve as **indentured** laborers. But disease, especially yellow fever, decimated the European population.

During the 1720s, about 6,000 African-born slaves were imported to colonial Louisiana. They had immunity to yellow fever. Most worked on plantations along the Mississippi River. By the early 1730s, slaves born in Africa made up about 65 percent of Louisiana's population.

Voodoo was a folk religion that became popular among slaves in Louisiana during the 18th and 19th centuries. It blended West African tribal religions with the Roman Catholicism of the French colonists. This is the tomb of Marie Laveau, a legendary New Orleans Voodoo queen. (The XXX markings were left by people asking her spirit to help them with problems.)

From the mid-1740s to the mid-1750s, colonial Louisiana enjoyed a measure of prosperity, despite frequent conflicts with Indians. The population was bolstered by arrivals from France. Plantations became more profitable with the importation of additional slaves from the islands of the French West Indies.

In the early 1800s, President Thomas Jefferson offered to buy the city of New Orleans from France. Instead, the United States wound up purchasing the entire Louisiana Territory in 1803.

But then came the Seven Years' War. In the late stages of the conflict, the French convinced Spain to become an ally in the fight against Great Britain. In return, a secret treaty signed in 1762 promised Spain all of the huge territory of French Louisiana. By 1763, however, France was defeated. In the treaty ending the Seven Years' War, France ceded to Great Britain its territory east of the Mississippi River, with the exception of New Orleans. Thus, the British took possession of the southeastern corner of the present-day state of Louisiana. The Spanish took possession of the rest.

The Seven Years' War had another important consequence for Louisiana.

During the war, the British expelled the French-speaking Acadian people living in Nova Scotia, New Brunswick, and Prince Edward Island (in present-day eastern Canada). Eventually, thousands of Acadians settled in southern Louisiana, where their descendants developed the unique Cajun culture.

At first, French colonists in Louisiana chafed at Spanish rule. In 1768, the Spanish governor was overthrown in a popular revolt. The next year, Spain sent a large force to Louisiana and regained control. Over the following decades, several thousand Spanish people settled in Louisiana.

In 1800, Spain and France signed a secret treaty. It returned the territory of Louisiana to France. But Spain was to keep governing until France was ready to take possession. In 1803, the French ruler Napoleon Bonaparte decided to sell Louisiana to the United States instead. The Louisiana Purchase roughly doubled the size of the United States.

In 1804, the Territory of Orleans was organized. It included all of present-day Louisiana except the area east of the Mississippi River. That had belonged to Spain since 1783, but it was not part of the Louisiana Purchase. In 1810, however, the United States annexed this area and made it part of the Territory of Orleans.

On April 30, 1812, Louisiana achieved statehood. It was the 18th state admitted to the Union.

In the decades that followed, Louisiana prospered. Planters grew wealthy cultivating sugar and cotton. Americans flocked to Louisiana from other states. Large numbers of immigrants arrived from Ireland and Germany. New Orleans became a center of commerce and the busiest port in the South.

By 1860, Louisiana had a total population of 708,000, including more than 330,000 slaves. But Louisiana was also home to nearly 19,000 free blacks. Many of them were the descendants of Haitians who'd arrived in the last decade of the 18th century or the first decade of the 19th. Most of them lived in or around New Orleans.

The Battle of New Orleans was the last major clash between American and British troops during the War of 1812. This painting shows General Andrew Jackson exhorting his men to repel the invading British. The battle was an American victory, and made Jackson a national hero. He would be elected president of the United States in 1828.

Before the Civil War, Louisiana had many grand plantation estates. One that has survived is historic Nottoway Plantation, located near White Castle. The mansion has been restored, and is open for tours and special events.

In early 1862, General Benjamin F. Butler (1818–1893) was appointed commander of the Union troops that occupied New Orleans during the Civil War. He ruled the territory with an iron hand, invoking the hatred of Southerners and earning the nickname "Beast Butler."

Louisiana seceded from the Union in January 1861. After two months as an independent republic, it joined the Confederacy.

More than 50,000 Louisianans fought for the Confederate cause. But nearly 30,000—more than 5,000 whites and 24,000 blacks—took up arms for the Union. Federal troops were able to occupy much of Louisiana after a Union naval force under the command of David Farragut steamed up the Mississippi River and captured New Orleans in April 1862.

After the war, political developments in Louisiana—especially in the matter of race relations—took a similar course to what occurred in Alabama and other states in the South. The advancement of African Americans' rights during Reconstruction was soon halted. Jim Crow segregation took hold in the late 1800s and lasted until the civil rights movement of the 1950s and 1960s.

During the 20th century, New Orleans took its place as an American cultural treasure. In the first decades of the 1900s, the city gave birth to a new kind of music: jazz.

On August 29, 2005, Hurricane Katrina wreaked havoc throughout the

A condemned home and debris lies in a street of New Orleans' Ninth Ward in the aftermath of Hurricane Katrina. The August 2005 storm devastated the Gulf Coast, killing more than 1,800 people and causing over $80 billion in damage. Many of the deaths occurred in New Orleans, as the failure of levees resulted in catastrophic flooding throughout more than three-quarters of the city.

A band performs zydeco music at a festival. Zydeco is a form of music native to southwest Louisiana. It developed out of the Cajun culture, and blends traditional Cajun music with blues, R&B, brass, and other styles.

Gulf Coast region. But the hurricane hit New Orleans especially hard. Much of the city sits below sea level. Only a system of levees (embankments) keeps the waters of the Mississippi River and Lake Pontchartrain out. The hurricane breached the levees, flooding about 80 percent of the city. In some places, the floodwaters reached 20 feet deep. More than a thousand people are believed to have died in New Orleans, and several hundred elsewhere in Louisiana. Hundreds of thousands were left homeless by the disaster.

Government

Louisiana's bicameral state legislature consists of the 105-seat House of Representatives and the 39-seat Senate. Members of both chambers serve four-year terms. Both chambers have term limits. Representatives and senators may serve no more than three consecutive terms.

The Louisiana State Legislature is a part-time body. Regular legislative business can be conducted on no more than 60 days in even-numbered years, and 45 days in odd-numbered years.

Louisianans elect their governor to a four-year term. Governors are limited to two consecutive terms.

Besides its two U.S. senators, Louisiana's delegation to the United States Congress includes six members of the House of Representatives.

Huey P. Long (1893–1935) drew national attention as the populist governor of Louisiana from 1928 to 1932. "The Kingfish" then served in the U.S. Senate from 1932 until the relative of a political rival shot and killed him in 1935.

Louisiana's state capitol building includes a tower rising 450 feet (137 m), making it the tallest capitol building in the United States. The building in Baton Rouge has chambers where the state legislature meets, as well as offices for the governor and his staff.

The Economy

Louisiana has substantial natural resources. It claims more than 9 percent of known U.S. oil reserves, mostly in the Gulf of Mexico. It also ranks among the top U.S. states in the production of natural gas, sulfur, and salt.

With 16 oil refineries, Louisiana is among the top states in gasoline production. Its large petrochemical industry churns out fertilizers, plastics, and other products.

Louisiana's top agricultural products include rice, cotton, sugarcane, and sweet potatoes. The state also produces beef cattle.

An oil refinery in Chalmette. Louisiana has the greatest concentration of crude oil refineries, natural gas processing plants, and petrochemical production facilities in the Western Hemisphere.

Alligators are bred and raised on this Louisiana farm, then killed to produce meat, leather, and other goods. Alligator farms actually help conservation of wild alligators, as they reduce poaching by providing a legal way to access goods made from alligator hide.

Commercial fishing is a major industry. Louisiana is the top producer of shrimp and oysters in the United States.

Tourism is another mainstay of Louisiana's economy, and New Orleans leads the way. More than 9 million people visited the city in 2012, pumping about $6 billion into the local economy.

According to recent data from the U.S. Census Bureau, Louisiana ranks 42nd among the 50 states in income per person.

The People

As far as population goes, Louisiana falls right in the middle: 25th out of 50. The U.S. Census Bureau estimates that the state has about 4.65 million residents.

Louisiana's population includes a much smaller proportion of whites (63.7 percent) than are in the country as a whole (77.9 percent). It has a much higher proportion of African Americans (32.4 percent versus 13.1 percent). Just 4.5 percent of Louisianans are of Latino ancestry,

 Did You Know?

Cajun French, a dialect that developed from the French spoken by Acadians and other early French settlers, is still widely spoken in southern Louisiana. Louisiana Creole also continues to be spoken in that region. It combines French and elements of West African tongues, with borrowings from Spanish and Native American languages.

compared with nearly 17 percent nationwide.

But the Census Bureau's categories are hardly adequate in conveying Louisiana's ethnic and cultural diversity. The evidence of that diversity is everywhere. It can be seen in a New Orleans parade—whether based on the French tradition of Mardi Gras or the Irish celebration of St. Patrick's Day. It can be heard in the accordian-driven zydeco music of black *Creoles* or in the clipped speech of Cajuns. It can be tasted in gumbo or jambalaya or tamales and salsa.

Some Famous Louisianans

Born on a Louisiana plantation, Confederate general P. G. T. Beauregard (1818–1893) ordered the bombardment of Fort Sumter, the first shots of the Civil War.

Louis Armstrong (1901–1971) was one of jazz's founding fathers. Fellow New Orleans trumpeters Al Hirt (1922–1999) and Wynton Marsalis (b. 1961) are among the many to follow in his footsteps.

Singer Mahalia Jackson (1911–1972), known as "the Queen of Gospel," was a native of New Orleans.

Ellen DeGeneres

Comedian, actress, and talk-show host Ellen DeGeneres (b. 1958) was born and raised in Metairie. Musician and reality show judge Randy Jackson (b. 1956) grew up in Baton Rouge.

Peyton Manning (b. 1976) and Eli Manning (b. 1981) have both quarterbacked NFL teams to Super Bowl championships. The brothers grew up in New Orleans. Eli's teammate with the Giants, receiver Odell Beckham (b. 1992), was born in Baton Rouge and played football at Louisiana State University.

Peyton Manning

Actress Reese Witherspoon (b. 1976) was a native of New Orleans before she was "legally blonde."

Louis Armstrong statue in New Orleans.

Reese Witherspoon

After the devastation of Hurricane Katrina, Americans wondered if New Orleans could ever recover. However, through hard work homes and businesses were rebuilt and people soon began returning to the city.

Major Cities

Nicknamed the Crescent City and the Big Easy, **New Orleans** is a major port and commercial center. It's more famous, though, for its historic French Quarter, annual Mardi Gras celebration, and great music and food. Hurricane Katrina devastated the city in August 2005, and New Orleans continues to rebuild. With an estimat-

An aerial view of Baton Rouge, the capital of Louisiana. It is the state's second-largest city, and is a major center of industry and business.

ed 2014 population of close to 370,000, the Big Easy is Louisiana's largest city. Yet it's still nowhere close to its pre-Katrina population of about 485,000.

Louisiana's capital, **Baton Rouge**, is located on the eastern bank of the Mississippi River, about 75 miles (121 km) northwest of New Orleans. Baton Rouge (French for "red staff") was founded in 1719. Today, it's home to about 230,000 people.

Shreveport, a city of more than 200,000, sits along the Red River in northwestern Louisiana's Caddo and Bossier parishes. Among its attractions are riverboat casinos.

A suburb of New Orleans, **Metairie** is located on the south shore of Lake Pontchartrain. About 140,000 people live in this city.

Lafayette, a city of more than 120,000 in the southern parish of the same name, bills itself as "the Heart of Cajun Country."

Further Reading

Freedman, Jeri. *Louisiana: Past and Present*. New York: Rosen Publishing Group, 2010.

Gessler, Diana Hollingsworth. *Very New Orleans: A Celebration of History, Culture, and Cajun Charm*. Chapel Hill, NC: Algonquin Books, 2006.

Macaulay, Ellen. *Louisiana (From Sea to Shining Sea, Second Series)*. New York: Scholastic, 2009.

Internet Resources

http://www.knowla.org/

Home page of KnowLA, an online encyclopedia of Louisiana history and culture.

http://www.louisianafolklife.org/LT/Articles_Essays/creole_art_creole_state.html

A brief introduction to Louisiana's traditional culture.

http://www.louisianatravel.com/

Photos, video, and other information from Louisiana's travel authority.

 # Text-Dependent Questions

1. Where did the Cajuns come from?
2. Name the three European countries that controlled all or part of Louisiana before the United States.
3. What style of music is New Orleans especially known for?

 # Research Project

Over the past few decades, Louisiana has steadily been losing coastal wetlands. An area the size of a football field disappears every hour. Find out why this has been happening, what can be done to stop it, and why wetlands are important.

Mississippi
at a Glance

Area: 48,432 sq mi (125,438 sq km)[1]
  32nd largest state
  Land: 46,923 sq mi (121,530 sq km)
  Water: 1,509 sq mi (3,908 sq km)
Highest elevation: Woodall
  Mountain, 806 feet (246 m)
Lowest elevation: Gulf of Mexico,
  sea level

Statehood: December 10, 1817
  (20th state)
Capital: Jackson

Population: 2,994,079
  (31st largest state)[2]

State nickname: the Magnolia State
State bird: mockingbird
State flower: magnolia

[1] *U.S. Census Bureau*
[2] *U.S. Census Bureau, 2014 estimate*

Mississippi

The Rolling Stones, Led Zeppelin, and Eric Clapton are among the legends of rock and roll. They all come from England. But if you listen closely to their music, you can hear the unmistakable influence of a different place: the Mississippi Delta. In this area of western Mississippi, hardship and a sorrowful history gave rise to the blues. And blues music, in turn, helped spawn rock and roll.

Geography

Covering more than 48,000 square miles (125,000 sq km), Mississippi is the 32nd largest state by area. It has borders with four other states. Louisiana is to the south and west, with Arkansas forming the rest of Mississippi's western border. Tennessee borders Mississippi to the north, and Alabama to the east. Mississippi has 44 miles (71 km) of coastline on the Gulf of Mexico. Five barrier islands in the Gulf also belong to Mississippi.

Most of Mississippi is made up of coastal plain. In the south-eastern part of the state, by the Gulf of Mexico, the land is low

The alluvial plain of the Mississippi River dominates the western part of the state. In the northwest is a football-shaped floodplain bounded by the Mississippi and Yazoo rivers. About 70 miles (113 km) at its widest, the area extends some 200 miles (322 km) from north to south. This is the famed Mississippi Delta, and it has some of the richest soil in the entire world. (It shouldn't be confused with the Mississippi River delta, in southeastern Louisiana.) The Mississippi Delta has been intensely farmed since the 1800s. It has few trees. Much of the rest of the state remains heavily forested.

and flat. But small, rolling hills cover much of the center of the state. Arcing across the coastal plain, from Alcorn County in the north through Noxubee County on the eastern border with Alabama, is the fertile Black Belt.

Words to Understand in This Chapter

annexation—the act of taking territory and incorporating it into a country or state.

campaign—in war, a connected series of military operations.

lynch—to kill someone by mob action.

sharecropping—an arrangement by which a farmer works land owned by another person, in exchange for a share of profits from the harvest.

siege—the military encirclement of a city or other position in order to cut off the enemy's supplies and force surrender.

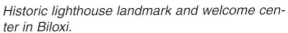
Historic lighthouse landmark and welcome center in Biloxi.

Magnolia trees bloom in a park. The magnolia is the state tree of Mississippi.

A swamp in fall along the Natchez Trace Parkway.

Aerial view of barges on the Mississippi River.

Besides the Mississippi and Yazoo, Mississippi's major rivers include the Pearl and the Big Black. Mississippi's largest lakes—Arkabutla Lake, Grenada Lake, Ross Barnett Reservoir, and Sardis Lake—are all manmade. With a surface area of nearly 155 square miles (400 sq km), Sardis Lake is the largest. It was formed by a dam on the Little Tallahatchie River.

Mississippi has a warm, humid climate, with minimal variation across the state. Winters are mild. Statewide, January daily lows average 31°F (–1°C), and January daily highs average 53°F (12°C). On a typical July day, temperatures will climb from around 71°F (22°C) to around 92°F (33°C). Average annual precipitation is nearly 60 inches (152 cm). Some areas in northern Mississippi get a

Emerald Mound is a Native American ceremonial site located near present-day Stanton. It was built by ancestors of the Natchez people, who encountered the first Europeans that arrived in the region during the 16th century.

couple inches of snowfall in a typical year, but snow is rare in most of the state.

History

Hernando de Soto's expedition crossed through what is today Mississippi in 1540–1541. Among the native peoples they encountered there were the Chickasaw and the Natchez.

In 1699, the French built Fort Maurepas on the eastern shore of Biloxi Bay, at present-day Ocean Springs, Mississippi. The settlement, also known as Old Biloxi, was abandoned 20 years later when sand bars made it difficult for ships to reach. Another settlement, New Biloxi— today simply called Biloxi—was constructed across the bay. It served as the capital of French Louisiana between 1720 and 1722.

In late 1729 and 1730, the French battled and ultimately defeated the Natchez Indians in what is today southwestern Mississippi. Many Natchez were killed. Many others were captured and sold into slavery. Most of those who avoided either fate

In 1539, the Spanish explorer Hernando de Soto landed with a small army somewhere on the coast of Florida. Over the next four years de Soto and his men explored a large portion of the southeastern United States, including Alabama and Mississippi, hoping to find gold.

found refuge with other tribes. The French mounted two **campaigns** against the Chickasaw during the 1730s. But both campaigns ended in disaster for the French.

In 1763, Great Britain took control of the Gulf Coast region east of the

 Did You Know?

In 1969, Hurricane Camille cut a channel through Mississippi's Ship Island, creating East Ship Island and West Ship Island. In 2005, Hurricane Katrina caused significant damage to both of these barrier islands.

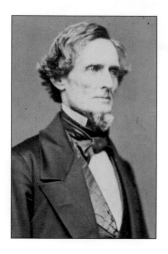

Jefferson Davis (1808–1889) served as U.S. Secretary of War from 1853 to 1857, and represented Mississippi in the U.S. Senate from 1857 to 1861. He resigned his senate seat when Mississippi voted to secede, and was subsequently elected president of the Confederate States of America in 1861.

Mississippi River after the Seven Years' War. The British promoted settlement in the Natchez District—what is today the southwestern corner of Mississippi. During the early years of the Revolutionary War, the Natchez District saw an influx of American colonists who remained loyal to the British king. But in 1779, a Spanish force seized the area.

The 1783 Treaty of Paris, which formally ended the Revolutionary War, left the newly independent United States in control of most of present-day Mississippi. Spain kept control of the southern part. The United States would later claim the rest of Mississippi by treaty and by ***annexation***.

The Mississippi Territory, which included a sliver of the present-day states of Mississippi and Alabama, was organized in 1798. The territory's boundaries were expanded in 1804 and again in 1812.

In 1817, Mississippi gained statehood. It was the 20th state admitted to the Union.

Mississippi's non-Indian population stood at about 75,000 in 1820. That number had surpassed 136,000 by 1830, the year President Andrew Jackson signed into law the Indian Removal Act. A decade later, with Indians forced from their land, Mississippi's population had doubled, to 375,000. Of this number, more than half—about 195,000—were slaves. But in counties where cotton plantations abounded—particularly in the Natchez area, across the Black Belt, and in parts of the Mississippi Delta—slaves often outnumbered the free population by more than five to one. The city of Natchez had a booming slave market and was home to

The fall of Vicksburg on July 4, 1863, was a major blow to the Confederacy. Although it is often overshadowed by the Battle of Gettysburg, which concluded the day before, the capture of Vicksburg gave Union forces effective control of the Mississippi, making it extremely hard for Confederate troops to receive the supplies they needed to keep fighting. Today, tens of thousands of people visit Vicksburg National Military Park each year.

some of the richest cotton planters in the South.

By 1860, Mississippi's population topped 791,000, including some 437,000 slaves. Free blacks in Mississippi numbered only about 1,000. This was mostly because the state legislature had passed laws to prevent slave owners from freeing slaves.

On January 9, 1861, Mississippi became the second state (after South Carolina) to secede from the Union. When the Confederate States of America was founded in February,

Mississippi's Jefferson Davis was chosen to serve as its president. Nearly 80,000 of his fellow Mississippians would fight for the Confederacy during the Civil War.

Much fighting occurred on Mississippi soil. Major battles took place at Corinth, Iuka, Raymond, and Meridian. But the most significant struggle was for Vicksburg. The town was situated on a bluff overlooking the Mississippi River. As long as it—and the downriver town of Port Hudson, Louisiana—remained in Confederate hands, Confederate forces could use the river to move supplies. For six weeks, Union troops laid *siege* to Vicksburg. Finally, on July 4, 1863, the Confederate defenders surrendered. Port Hudson fell five days later.

Mississippi's economy was in tatters at the end of the Civil War. Its society was even more unsettled. Newly free African Americans made up 55 percent of the state's population. Yet whites seemed determined to prevent them from gaining equality. Mississippi's whites, one federal official observed, "still have an ingrained feeling that the blacks at large belong to the whites at large."

Mississippi's legislature passed laws limiting the rights of black people. The Ku Klux Klan, a racist organization that operated throughout the South, terrorized African Americans. Many blacks were *lynched*.

Many of Mississippi's white planters were impoverished and had to sell their land. But they refused to sell land to African Americans, even if that meant selling to white buyers at half the price. By 1870, when Mississippi was readmitted into the Union, *sharecropping* had become common. Under this arrangement, a landowner assigned a black (or poor white) family a small parcel of land to farm. The family and the landowner split the profits from the crops that were grown—but only after the landowner had deducted the cost of equipment, seeds, and other items he'd provided. Sharecropping kept many thousands of African Americans in desperate poverty.

An exception to this bleak situation, at least for a while, existed in the Mississippi Delta region. Much of the land there had never been cleared and cultivated. So African Americans were able to acquire their own farmland in the Delta after the Civil War.

 Did You Know?

The Thirteenth Amendment to the Constitution, which banned slavery, went into effect in December 1865. But Mississippi didn't officially ratify the amendment until February 2013.

James Meredith walks to class at the University of Mississippi, accompanied by federal marshals, October 1962.

Unfortunately, cotton prices bottomed out in the 1870s and remained low through the 1890s. This plunged Delta farmers into debt. Most were forced to sell their land and become sharecroppers. The Delta has been an area of high poverty ever since.

Poor economic conditions, Jim Crow laws, and the constant threat of racial violence continued to make life difficult for Mississippi's African Americans in the 20th century. Between about 1910 and 1970, more than 300,000 black Mississippians joined in what became known as the Great Migration. This was a massive movement of African Americans from the South to cities in the northern and western parts of the country.

Mississippi was a major battleground in the struggle for civil rights. In 1962, violent riots broke out on the Oxford campus of the all-white University of Mississippi when an African-American student named James Meredith enrolled there. Ultimately, federal troops were called in to quell the unrest. In 1963, civil rights leader Medgar Evers was assassinated in Jackson. The following year, members of the Ku Klux Klan murdered three civil rights workers near

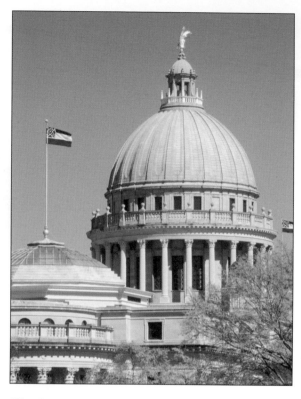

The flag of Mississippi flies over the State Capitol building in Jackson.

the Mississippi town of Philadelphia. In the end, though, outrage at the violence helped lead to the passage of the Civil Rights Act of 1964.

Government

The Mississippi Legislature consists of the 122-seat House of Representatives and the 52-seat Senate. Representatives are elected to two-year terms, whereas senators are elected to four-year terms. There are no limits on how many terms a person may serve in either chamber.

Term limits do apply to Mississippi's governor, however. No one may serve more than two four-year terms as governor. That rule applies whether or not the terms are consecutive.

Mississippi's delegation to the U.S. Congress includes four members of the House of Representatives. As of 2015, three of them—in addition to both of Mississippi's U.S. senators—were Republicans. This reflects the state's conservative politics. Research conducted by the Gallup Organization in 2012 found Mississippi to be the fourth most conservative state in the country.

The Economy

By most measures, Mississippi is the poorest state in the country. In income per person, for example, Mississippians fall more than 25 percent below the national average.

A shrimp boat fishes the waters near Biloxi. Shrimp fishing is an important part of the state's seafood industry.

Casinos and hotels overlook the Gulf at sunset. Mississippi legalized casino gambling in 1990, and since then it has been one of the leading states with regard to gaming revenue.

Some Famous Mississippians

Jefferson Davis (1808–1889) was a soldier and U.S. senator from Mississippi before becoming president of the Confederate States of America.

Nobel Prize–winning writer William Faulkner (1897–1962) was a longtime resident of Oxford.

Mississippi has produced many of the country's greatest blues musicians. A partial list includes Robert Johnson (1911–1938), whose guitar playing was so astounding he was said to have sold his soul to the devil; Muddy Waters (1913–1983), considered the founding father of the Chicago style of blues; and B. B. King (b. 1925), perhaps the most influential of all blues artists.

William Faulkner

Despite his name, Tennessee Williams (1911–1983) was a native of Mississippi. He's considered one of America's greatest play-wrights.

Elvis Presley (1935–1977), "the King of Rock and Roll," was the pride of Tupelo. Pop singers Britney Spears (b. 1981) and Brandy Norwood (b. 1979) were both born in McComb. Country music star Faith Hill (b. 1967), who grew up in Mississippi, has sold more than 40 million albums.

Generations of American kids have learned their ABCs thanks to Jim Henson (1936–1990), creator of the Muppets. Henson was born in Greenville.

Fannie Hamer

Talk-show host, actress, and television producer Oprah Winfrey (b. 1954) was born in Kosciusko.

In 1964 civil rights activist Fannie Lou Hamer (1917–1977) helped to create the Mississippi Freedom Democratic Party (MFDP) and encouraged African Americans to vote.

Running back Walter Payton (1954–1999), wide receiver Jerry Rice (b. 1962), and quarterback Brett Favre (b. 1969) all went from Mississippi to storied careers in the NFL.

Brett Favre

Agriculture continues to play a major role in Mississippi's economy. Every year, Mississippi ranks among the top two or three states in cotton production. Other important crops include soybeans and rice.

Mississippi has a significant commercial seafood industry. Shrimp and oysters are caught in the Gulf of Mexico. Mississippi is also a leading producer of farm-raised catfish.

The Japanese car companies Toyota and Nissan both have large factories in Mississippi. Mississippi-based auto-parts manufacturers help keep their assembly lines running.

Aircraft parts are also manufactured in Mississippi. Other important manufactured products include furniture, chemicals, and processed foods.

The People

By population, Mississippi is the 31st largest state. The U.S. Census Bureau estimated that there were nearly 3 million Mississippians in 2014.

Before the Great Migration, African Americans outnumbered whites in Mississippi. Today, Mississippi still has a higher proportion of blacks than any other state—37.4 percent, according to the U.S. Census Bureau. Six in 10

The University of Southern Mississippi, located near Hattiesburg, enrolls more than 15,000 students.

A view of downtown Jackson. The capital is also the state's largest city.

Mississippians, meanwhile, are white.

Mississippi is home to much smaller percentages of Asian Americans and Latinos than the country overall. More than 5 percent of the people in the United States are of Asian ancestry. In Mississippi, that figure is less than 1 percent. Similarly, while nearly 17 percent of Americans are Latinos, less than 3 percent of Mississippians are.

The Magnolia State isn't a magnet for immigrants. According to the Census Bureau, just 2.2 percent of Mississippi residents were born in a foreign country. That compares with a

The Hurricane Katrina Memorial at Biloxi was erected a year after the superstorm caused severe damage to much of the Gulf Coast in August 2005. Biloxi, Gulfport, and other coastal towns were badly damaged by flooding and high winds. More than a million Mississippians were displaced from their homes, and 235 died.

figure of 12.9 percent for the United States as a whole.

Major Cities

Mississippi has only one city with a population of more than 100,000. That city is *Jackson*, home to about 175,000 people. Jackson has served as the state capital since 1822. It's located mostly in west-central Hinds County, on the eastern bank of the Pearl River.

With casino gambling and more than six miles (10 km) of beaches on the Gulf of Mexico, *Gulfport* is a tourist destination. The city's 2010 population stood at close to 68,000.

Southhaven is located in northwestern DeSoto County, right on the border with Tennessee. It's considered a suburb of Memphis, which is about 15 miles (24 km) to the north, and has a population of about 50,000.

Hattiesburg, the county seat of southern Mississippi's Forrest County, developed in the late 1800s as a railroad hub. It has a population of about 46,000.

Further Reading

Ballard, Michael B. *Civil War Mississippi: A Guide.* Jackson: University Press of Mississippi, 2000.

Gaines, Ann. *Mississippi (It's My State).* New York: Cavendish Square Publishing, 2014.

Somervill, Barbara A. *Mississippi.* New York: Scholastic, 2009.

Internet Resources

http://mshistorynow.mdah.state.ms.us/

Mississippi History Now, an online publication of the Mississippi Historical Society, offers articles on a wide range of topics related to the state.

http://www.pbs.org/theblues/roadtrip/deltahist.html

Online resources examining the Delta style of blues music, from PBS.

http://www.visitmississippi.org/

The Web site of Mississippi's tourism agency.

 # Text-Dependent Questions

1. Which two rivers form the boundaries of the Mississippi Delta?
2. Name the Mississippian who became the president of the Confederate States of America in 1861.
3. What is a sharecropper?

 # Research Project

Choose a blues musician from Mississippi. Read about the person's life, and write a one-page report.

Index

Numbers in **bold italics** refer to captions.

Series Glossary of Key Terms

bicameral—having two legislative chambers (for example, a senate and a house of representatives).

cede—to yield or give up land, usually through a treaty or other formal agreement.

census—an official population count.

constitution—a written document that embodies the rules of a government.

delegation—a group of persons chosen to represent others.

elevation—height above sea level.

legislature—a lawmaking body.

precipitation—rain and snow.

term limit—a legal restriction on how many consecutive terms an office holder may serve.